Looking at Science
How Things Change

Looking at

EARTH

HOW DOES IT CHANGE?

Jackie Gaff

Enslow Elementary

an imprint of

 Enslow Publishers, Inc.

40 Industrial Road
Box 398
Berkeley Heights, NJ 07922
USA

http://www.enslow.com

Enslow Elementary, an imprint of Enslow Publishers, Inc.

Enslow Elementary® is a registered trademark of Enslow Publishers, Inc.

This edition published in 2008 by Enslow Publishers, Inc.

Copyright © 2008 The Brown Reference Group plc

Library of Congress Cataloging-in-Publication Data

Gaff, Jackie
  Looking at earth : how does it change? / Jackie Gaff.
    p. cm. — (Looking at science : how things change)
  Summary: "Provides a look at Earth, its relationship to the sun, earthquakes,
volcanoes, and how people can help the planet"—Provided by publisher.
  Includes bibliographical references and index.
  ISBN-13: 978-0-7660-3088-6
  ISBN-10: 0-7660-3088-1
  1. Earth—Juvenile literature. I. Title.
  QB631.4.G34 2008
  550—dc22

2007024507

Printed in the United States of America

10 9 8 7 6 5 4 3 2 1

To Our Readers: We have done our best to make sure all Internet Addresses in this book were active and appropriate when we went to press. However, the author and the publisher have no control over and assume no liability for the material available on those Internet sites or on other Web sites they may link to. Any comments or suggestions can be sent by e-mail to comments@enslow.com or to the address on the back cover.

Every effort has been made to locate all copyright holders of material used in this book. If any errors or omissions have occurred, corrections will be made in future editions of this book.

For The Brown Reference Group plc
Project Editor: Sarah Eason
Designer: Paul Myerscough
Picture Researcher: Maria Joannou
Children's Publisher: Anne O'Daly

Photo and Illustration Credits: The Brown Reference Group plc (illustrations), pp. 8, 10, 14–15; Corbis/Noburu Hashimoto, p. 12, Corbis/Jose Luis Pelaez, Inc, p. 25T; Dreamstime, pp. 8, 16; istockphoto, pp. 6, 17, 18, 20, 22L, 22R, 24, 28, 28B, 29T; NASA, pp. 4, 16B; Science Photo Library/Pascal, p. 11, Science Photo Library/Peter Menzell, p. 14B; Shutterstock, pp. 1, 2, 5, 9, 10, 12B, 15, 18B, 23T, 26, 27, 30; Geoff Ward (illustrations), pp. 7, 19, 21T, 21B, 24.
Cover Photo: Shutterstock

Contents

What is Earth?

Earth is the planet that we live on. Planets are huge masses that travel around a star. Some planets, like Earth, are made of mostly rock. Others are mostly gas.

North Pole

An imaginary line around the middle of Earth is called the equator.

South Pole

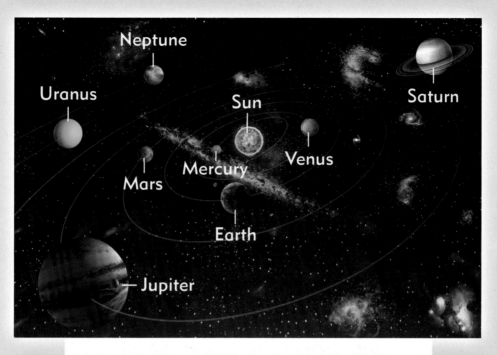

▲ Our solar system includes the Sun and the planets that move around it, as well as other matter such as asteroids. Solar means "of the Sun."

Earth is one of eight major planets that travel around the star that we call the Sun. Earth takes one year to orbit, or make a complete trip around, the Sun.

Why is Earth special?

Earth is the only planet in the solar system that we know has life. Earth has liquid water, which keeps animals and plants alive.

Tropical rainforests are ▶ very warm and wet. More than half of Earth's animals and plants live in rainforests.

This diagram ▶ shows the eight major planets in order from the Sun.

If Earth were nearer to the Sun, all of its water would boil away. If Earth were farther from the Sun, all of its water would freeze into ice.

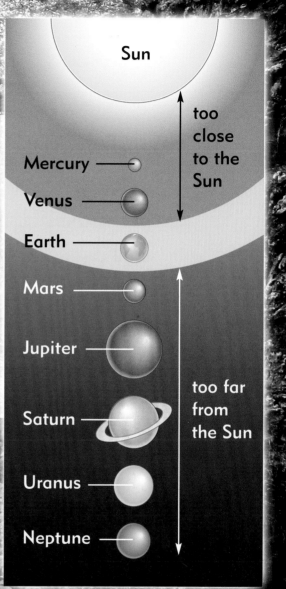

Sun

Mercury

Venus

Earth

Mars

Jupiter

Saturn

Uranus

Neptune

too close to the Sun

too far from the Sun

What is Earth made of?

Earth is made of mostly rock and metal. It has four layers. The layer that makes up Earth's surface is called its crust.

Earth's outer core is made of liquid metal.

Earth's crust is made of mostly solid rock.

Earth's inner core is made of solid metal.

The mantle is the thickest of all Earth's layers.

▼ Earth gets hotter towards its center.
Earth's inner core is at least 7,000 °F!

The layer below Earth's crust
is called the mantle. Beneath
the mantle is the outer core.
Within that is the inner core.

▲ Some of the rock that makes up
Earth's mantle layer is so hot that
it has melted and become liquid.

Does Earth change?

Yes! Earth is always changing. Earth's land and oceans change shape. Its plants and animals also change over time.

The dinosaurs died out about 65 million years ago, long before the earliest humans lived on Earth.

▼ This desert was once green land. It has changed into desert over time as Earth's climate has changed.

Earth's weather changes from day to day or week to week. The climate, or pattern of weather over many years, also changes.

Scientists think the ▶ first humans lived in Africa about 2 million years ago. This model shows what they may have looked like.

What makes the ground move?

Earth's crust is not completely solid. This is why Earth's ground moves and its land changes shape.

▼ Mountains sometimes form when Earth's plates push against each other. The world's highest mountains are the Himalayas, in Asia.

Buildings may fall down when an earthquake shakes the ground. New buildings are often designed to stand up to the shock of an earthquake.

Imagine that Earth's crust is a giant eggshell, which has cracked into about 30 pieces called plates. The plates push or rub against each other all the time.

If two plates suddenly move against each other, the ground may shudder and shake. It may even crack open. That is an earthquake.

What are volcanoes?

A volcano is a mountain that has an open crater at the top. Hot, liquid rock pushes up through the volcano and out onto the surface. The hot rock is called magma. When the magma reaches Earth's surface, it is called lava.

◄ The world's largest volcano is Mauna Loa, in Hawaii. It is 11 miles (17 km) tall.

Magma and hot gases
blast upward and out
of the volcano.

The mouth of a volcano
is called a crater.

Melted lava flows
down the side of
the volcano.

▲ Mount St. Helens in the
state of Washington
erupted in May 1980.
The eruption blasted
1300 feet (400 m) off
the top of the mountain.

Magma and hot
gases build up inside
a giant hole called a
magma chamber.

How does water change Earth?

Water can be as powerful as an earthquake or a volcano. Water changes Earth slowly, over a long period of time.

▼ Water covers almost three-quarters of Earth's surface.

It took millions of years for the ▲ Colorado River to carve out the Grand Canyon, in Arizona.

▲ These amazing rock formations are near the Mexican coast. They were made as the ocean pounded against the cliffs, wearing them away.

As rivers flow to the sea, they can carve out valleys and deep canyons. As waves batter the coast, they can eat away at the coastline. This wearing away of land is called erosion.

Why does day change into night?

There are other kinds of changes on Earth. For example, do you know how day changes into night?

As Earth spins around, the ▶ Sun comes into view and seems to rise in the sky.

◀ The Moon does not give off its own light. We can see the Moon because light from the Sun bounces off the Moon's surface.

Earth spins round and round as it travels around the Sun. As it spins, it is daytime on the side that faces the Sun. It is night on the other side.

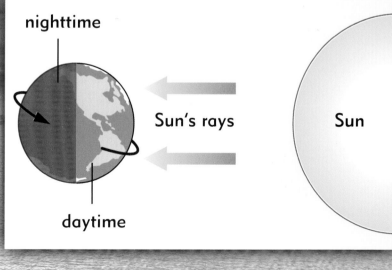

nighttime

Sun's rays

Sun

daytime

▲ Earth spins around once every 24 hours.

Why are there seasons?

Earth is tilted as it travels around the Sun. It "leans" in one direction. This helps create the seasons.

For one half of each year, the northern half of Earth leans toward the Sun and the southern half leans away.

For the other half of each year, the southern half of Earth leans toward the Sun. The northern half leans away.

Some birds will fly long ▲ distances to find warmer weather. They travel south when it is winter in the north. They return when it is winter in the south.

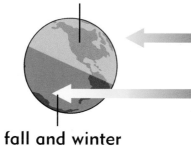

spring and summer

fall and winter

When the northern half of Earth is tilted toward the Sun, it has spring and summer. The southern half has fall and winter.

When the northern half is tilted away from the Sun, it has fall and winter. The southern half has spring and summer.

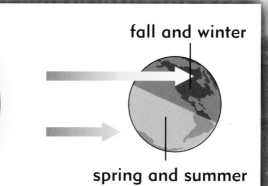

fall and winter

spring and summer

How do people use the Earth?

Did you know that sand is used to make glass?

We use the Earth in everyday life. Food is grown in Earth's soil. Materials from the ground or from plants and animals are used to make shelter or clothing.

Bricks are made out of clay found in soil.

Cotton is a plant. It is ▶
used to make clothes,
sheets, towels, and
other items.

Burning coal, oil,
or natural gas from
the Earth helps us to
make electricity. Many
tools are made from
metals that are dug
from the ground.

All of the materials that we
use from the Earth are called
natural resources.

Metal from the Earth is
used to make cars and
many other things.

How do people change Earth?

Every time we take something from Earth we change it. Some changes are small, such as cutting down a tree. Other changes are big, such as cutting down a whole forest.

▼ Gases in Earth's air, such as carbon dioxide, may be causing global warming. These gases are called greenhouse gases because they trap heat in the same way glass does in a greenhouse.

Trees take in carbon ▶ dioxide gas. Planting trees can help keep the air clean.

Making too much pollution and cutting down forests can change Earth's climate. Many people think Earth's climate may be getting too warm too fast. Global means "of the Earth," and we call the change in Earth's climate global warming.

Can people help protect Earth?

People should use Earth's natural resources carefully. For example, we burn fuel for energy. But burning fuels may cause global warming.

Here are some of the ways we use energy:

- Switching on a light, TV, or other household machines uses electricity.
- Taking a bath or shower uses fossil fuels, which are burned to heat the water.
- Traveling by car burns gasoline, which is made from oil.

If we use less energy, we may help to slow global warming.

Here are some of the ways we can save energy:
- Turn off lights and machines when they are not needed.
- Take quick showers instead of baths. Showers use less energy.
- Walk or bicycle instead of traveling by car.

What do I know about Earth?

1. Water, food, air, coal, oil, metals, wool, and cotton are natural resources.

How many natural resources do you think you use? Could you use fewer resources? Write down ways in which you think you could help to save Earth's resources.

2. Which resource do plants and animals need to live? Why does this resource make Earth so special?

3. Look up into the night sky. Can you see the Moon? Can you see any planets or stars?

4. Which season is it where you are now? What causes spring, summer, fall, or winter?

Words to Know

carbon dioxide — One of the gases found in air.

core — Earth's innermost layer of rock, found at its center.

crust — Earth's top layer of rock.

erosion — Wearing away of Earth's surface by weather.

equator — Imaginary line that runs around Earth's center.

global warming — Warming up of Earth's climate.

lava — Very hot rock that has melted.

mantle — Very thick layer of rock beneath Earth's crust.

natural resources — Materials, such as wood, that are found on Earth and can be used by people.

orbit — To travel around something.

planet — Mass of rock or gas that travels around a star.

seasons — Regular changes in weather and temperature caused by Earth's tilt as it orbits the Sun.

solar system — A star, such as the Sun, and the planets and other objects that orbit it.

year — The period of time it takes for a planet to orbit the Sun. Earth takes about 365 days to orbit the Sun.

Learn More

Books

Chancellor, Deborah. *Planet Earth*. Boston: Kingfisher (2006).

Davis, Kenneth C. *Don't Know Much About Planet Earth.*
New York: HarperTrophy (2001).

Caviezel, Giovanni. *Our Planet Earth*. New York:
Barron's (2003).

Web Sites

Geography for Kids
www.kidsgeo.com/geography-for-kids/0002-how-big-is-
the-earth.php

Earthquakes for Kids
http://earthquake.usgs.gov/learning/kids.php

Index

WITHDRAWN